LOVE HAIKU

Love Haiku

Japanese Poems of Yearning, Passion, and Remembrance

Translated and Edited by

PATRICIA DONEGAN *with* YOSHIE ISHIBASHI

Shambhala

BOSTON & LONDON

2010

Shambhala Publications, Inc.
Horticultural Hall
300 Massachusetts Avenue
Boston, Massachusetts 02115
www.shambhala.com

The illustrations in this book are from *Momoyogusa* (Flowers of a
Hundred Generations) by Sekka Kamisaka (1909). Spencer Collection,
The New York Public Library, Astor, Lenox, and Tilden Foundations.
Reproduced by permission.

Watermark on pages i, 1, 49, and 121: Stencil of *Grape Leaves on a Vertical
Striped Ground* (artist unknown, late 19th to early 20th c.). Santa Barbara
Museum of Art, gift of Mrs. Lockwood de Forest. Reprinted by permission.

9 8 7 6 5 4 3 2 1

FIRST EDITION

Printed in China

♾ This edition is printed on acid-free paper that meets the American
National Standards Institute z39.48 Standard.
♻ Shambhala Publications makes every effort to print on recycled paper.
For more information please visit www.shambhala.com.
Distributed in the United States by Random House, Inc.,
and in Canada by Random House of Canada Ltd

Designed by Michael Russem, Kat Ran Press

If you cannot fall in love, you cannot get enlightened.

CHÖGYAM TRUNGPA RINPOCHE

Contents

Acknowledgments

Gratitude to many

First, to Peter Turner, president of Shambhala Publications, who was enthusiastic about this book from the start. And to the founder, Sam Bercholz, who encouraged me to publish with Shambhala years ago.

To my editor of several books, Jennifer Urban-Brown, whose patient understanding and insightful and sharp editing helped make this a better book.

To all the Japanese haiku poets and their families who kindly gave us permission to use their haiku in this collection; without their beautiful haiku, this book could not exist. Also, a deep thanks to the Japan Writers' Association for the permission to reprint many of the poems here.

To Yoshie Ishibashi, dear friend, longtime collaborator, and insightful historical researcher as well as translator, whose dedicated contribution was invaluable. For this book, a special thanks for doing the permissions.

To Susan Edwards (1943–2008), loving friend, metaphysician, artist, and writer who cheered me on my writing path; she left so soon yet her lifetime sharing of her openheartedness and wisdom has been a blessing for me and for so many.

To William J. Higginson (1938–2008), haiku poet, scholar, and friend, whose untimely death leaves a gap in the haiku world, yet we are grateful to have his deep knowledge.

To the libraries of Northwestern University and the University of Chicago, for help with the Japanese biographies.

To all of those persons over my lifetime I have been fortunate to love and to be loved by, whether with passion or with compassion, whether in the ups or the downs of love—this book would have been impossible without them.

To my meditation teacher Chögyam Trungpa Rinpoche (1940–1987), who was not afraid to love passionately, who taught me the importance of that and of living fearlessly with a "broken heart," so that compassion is the ground for passion and for our daily life as well.

To my dear parents, Daniel Patrick Donegan and Janet Caroline Fries Donegan, whose love has guided and sustained me my whole life.

Special thanks to

Akito Arima; Atsushi Azumi and Kunio Azumi; Shoshi Fujita and Kaori Fujita; Takako Hashimoto and Miyoko Hashimoto; Kiyo Hinoki; Tatsuko Hoshino and Takashi Hoshino; Dakotsu Iida and Hidemi Iida; Sumiko Ikeda; Kikuno Inagaki and Sakurako Eida; Kanajo Hasegawa and Hiroshi Hasegawa; Hakyo Ishida and Shudai Ishida; Yatsuka Ishihara and Toshiki Ishihara; Tota Kaneko; Shuson Kato and Hodaka Kato; Nobuko Katsura and Takuma Niwa; Mantaro Kubota and the Kubota Mantaro Memorial Fund Committee; Momoko Kuroda; Takajo Mitsuhashi and Ayako Mitsuhashi; Shuoshi Mizuhara and Haruo Mizuhara; Sumio Mori; Koi Nagata and Ise Nagata; Takeo Nakajima and Hisako Nakajima; Kusatao Nakamura and Yumiko Nakamura; Sonoko Nakamura and Rinji Nakamura; Teijo Nakamura and Mamiko Ogawa; Toshiro Nomura and Kenzo Nomura; Seisensui Ogiwara and Kaiichi Ogiwara; Rinka Ono and Reiko Ono; Sanki Saito and Naoki Saito; Onifusa Sato and Miho Yamada; Seisui Shiihashi and Sueko Shiihashi; Suzuko Shinagawa; Masajo Suzuki and Kaku Motoyama; Mitsu Suzuki; Kyoshi Takahama and Tomoko Takahama; Suju Takano and Natsuko Osawa; Jushin (Shigenobu) Takayanagi and Fukiko Takayanagi; Hanjo

Takehara and Michiyo Takehara; Taniko Terai; Kiyoko Tsuda; Momoko Tsuji; Kiyoko Uda; Nanako Washitani; Mikajo Yagi and Akira Shimoyama; Seishi Yamaguchi and Kobe University; Ikuyo Yoshimura; Yoshiko Yoshino and Hajime Yoshino; Nobuko Yoshiya and Yukiko Yoshiya; to all those who helped Yoshie in contacting the haiku poets, especially the Association of Haiku Poets, Tsurumaro Hashizume, Yasumi Ishibashi, Emiko Miyashita, Asako Nishijima, Masami Sanuka, and Nanae Tamura.

Introduction

For human beings throughout history, love has been considered a mystery, for it is an emotional experience that is both transcendent and personal at the same time. Love is perhaps the most familiar yet most unknowable of our emotions. It can transport us beyond our ego and fill us with bliss and compassion, but it can also be a crucible of rawness, pain, and illusion. Particularly in an intimate relationship—be it romantic or everyday—love's power can magically expand our humanity. At its very best, passion is spacious, open, compassionate, and even joyful. Yet how ironic that, as imperfect human beings, we yearn for "perfect love," for it will always elude us—the experience of love, whether painful or joyful, is always perfectly imperfect; this is love's paradox.

Love in a close relationship can be what is often called "the fast path to enlightenment" because a love relationship is a mirror with no escape, reminding us of our hidden corners: the places where we are selfish, impatient, or unkind. In this sense—actually in every sense—love is essential for our spiritual growth. Chögyam Trungpa Rinpoche put it more strongly: "If you cannot fall in love, you cannot get enlightened." For it is this state of leaping into the chaos of love—of being open, uncertain, and vulnerable—that becomes a stepping-stone to our highest self. When we truly love another person, we "lose ourselves," or our self is somehow transcended—even in a moment of wild carnal desire, some tenderness for our beloved arises—and it cracks our heart open and changes us forever.

If we can remember the fragility of love and see our beloved through the lens of impermanence, appreciation naturally arises; in Japanese this is known as *mono no aware*, the beauty of the transitory, be it a flower or love itself. As with all of life, within the seed of love is the seed of sorrow and death, which heightens its poignancy. Through loving one other person with this "broken heart," we have the rare opportunity to learn to focus less on our self and more on others—and that is the beginning of "true" love.

Haiku is a Japanese form of poetry, containing seventeen syllables in three phrases in Japanese or usually three lines (of 5-7-5 syllables) in English. A fine haiku presents a crystalline moment of heightened awareness in simple imagery, traditionally using a *kigo* or season word from nature. However, the view of haiku as only harmonious nature poetry is erroneous. Though not as prevalent, there have been haiku about war, politics, religion, and even about love. There is always the human drama of love and hate—and the intertwining of them both in the red thread of love haiku.

Although Japanese poets have never created a genre called "love haiku," one exists within the haiku world, perhaps as a hidden genre. Sometimes it is found in the *senryu*—a cousin of haiku, a poetic form focusing on the social realm of human life instead of on nature. Traditionally in Japan, the theme of love was reserved for the ancient five-line *tanka* (*waka*) poetry. As expressed by Ki no Tsurayuki in his preface to the *Kokinshu* (the ninth-century imperial poetry anthology), poetry was not just rooted in nature but "has its root in the human heart." For centuries this older form was mostly dominated by courtesan women and used subjective emotional expression.

Later, when the haiku form first evolved, it was thought to be less emotional and more objective and emphasized nature as its theme. Yet early love haiku can be found here and there throughout the centuries. In the fifteenth and sixteenth centuries, there were some *renga* (linked verse) masters like Soin Nishiyama who wrote "A Hundred Love Links" in which each of the links used the theme of love. And in the seventeenth century, "love" is even found in some of master Basho's haiku (called *hokku* in his era). Yet, except for some of Basho's verses written as part of the *renga*, which included three or four "love verses" in a sequence of thirty-six links, or perhaps his verses written as part of his *haibun* (short prose piece with haiku), he and his predecessors didn't write individual love haiku in the modern sense.

In the early twentieth century, love was still more prevalent in the tanka poetry, as in the female poet Akiko Yosano's *Midaregami* (Tangled Hair) erotic poetry collection of 1901. Yet around that same time haiku poets were beginning to expand the tradition-based haiku form to include subjective elements of love and sensuality, especially with the appearance of female poet forerunners such as Hisajo Sugita, Takako Hashimoto, and Nobuko Katsura, and to some degree male poet forerunners such as Kusatao Nakamura, Sojo Hino, and Sanki Saito. The female poet Masajo Suzuki is perhaps best known for love haiku among these modern poets because more of her love poetry has been translated into English than the other haiku poets; this anthology intends to give readers a fuller historical picture with the inclusion of the love haiku of these forerunners as well as many other poets.

ABOUT THIS BOOK

The purpose of this anthology is not only to feature haiku, but also to use these love haiku as a vehicle for transformation, awakening, and opening the heart. This collection of haiku is intended to remind us of the seed of love existing within each of us this very moment. Because the act of "pausing" or the heightened "aha moment," is built into the haiku form itself, the reading of these love haiku gives us a chance to slow down and pause for a few breaths as we reflect on love. This practice of pausing, of being present to the moment, can carry over to our everyday life and create an opening for our mind to relax; in this space, appreciation of the different aspects of love in our lives can arise, whether it is the state of being with a present lover, the recollection of love lost, or the sitting alone with our cat or a glass of wine in anticipation of love. Reading each love haiku is a mini-meditation that prompts us to pause, and cultivates love within us, passionate love as well as compassion. Loving energy magnetizes love, and is the basis for attraction and connection to another. These small poems are "pausings for love," and are ways to remember that source of love within us.

This collection is centered on "passionate or romantic love," which may touch upon the erotic but doesn't include haiku that are directly erotic or graphic. Love has many faces. For simplicity's sake this collection is divided into three sections: (1) yearning, (2) passion, and (3) remembrance. Rather than a neat "beginning, middle, and end," which rarely occurs with love, these themes highlight the elusive nature of love—for in one afternoon, or even one moment, love can go from passion to remembrance to yearning and back again. And even though we desire and feel that love is eternal, its shape and moods are not constant, but ever-changing, fleeting, full of ups and downs, waxing and waning.

Though there are more anthologies of love haiku being published in Japan these days, very little is available in English;

hopefully this love haiku anthology will add to this effort. For this anthology of 147 love haiku, with the help of Yoshie Ishibashi for research and translation, I tried to present a balance of these seventy-one Japanese poets: selections of poets from traditional and modern times to those who are contemporary and living, including male and female, younger and older. However, there were limitations: I did not include any of the living poets considered to be of the so-called "younger generation" (under sixty years old) first because of space limitations, and also because there are so many fine traditional and older modern haiku poets whose beautiful love haiku have rarely or never been translated into English. Above all, I feel honored to be able to include all of these fine poets in our book and to receive their kind permission to include their work; I take full responsibility for any mistakes that might exist in the biographical information or in the haiku translations.

The process of choosing the haiku that I labeled as "love haiku" for this anthology was very subjective. Some of the haiku clearly pinpointed romantic or passionate love, whereas others were more open-ended, and portrayed loneliness, for example— and I used those haiku to reflect the lonely longing for love, which may or may not have been originally intended. So I took liberal poetic license for this book while trying to remain true to its purpose.

Translation is said to be like a kiss through a veil. Japanese is challenging because it relies so heavily upon subtlety and the power of suggestion, whereas English relies so much upon clarity and precision. My approach was to be faithful to the original, taking out nothing, adding nothing; to be clear but not to destroy the elusive. Unlike traditional nature haiku that emphasizes a precise heightened moment, the love haiku instead mostly present sketches or beautiful images to evoke a feeling—an evocative quality that reverberates, as does any good love poem. I hope that some of the emotional essence of this love poetry, which at its best taps into a transcendental truth or mystery that exists beyond the words of language, remains in these translations— that the kiss is still recognizable as a kiss.

In the presentation of the haiku, I have placed the order of the Japanese names in the English order of given name first and family name last. In addition, for those readers who would like to hear the rhythm of how the haiku sounds in Japanese, I have included the romanji under the English translation; the romanji provides the closest equivalent in rendering the sound of the Japanese pronunciation into the Roman alphabet of English.

This collection of love haiku is intended for anyone who has been touched by love or who yearns to be touched by love. These poems are universal windows of the heart common to all human beings no matter what our personal views or sexual orientation, for the haiku reflect the shared experience of our highest potential: the ability to love and be loved.

These dark and difficult times make us yearn even more for that elusive state of love. Humans remain an enigmatic mix: aggression and hate rage within us, as do the fires of love. But love is the saving grace: we will continue to survive if we nurture that innate seed of love within us—our ability to feel *for* another, to think *of* another before oneself, and to extend openheartedness *to* another. For by learning to love one person, we learn to love the many. This is our hope for survival, for peace, for happiness, for ecstasy: to open to love. These love haiku give us a chance to pause, and they remind us of the way.

PATRICIA DONEGAN

YEARNING

this evening's moon—
I gaze on it alone
then go to sleep

konna ni yoi tsuki wo hitori de mite neru

HOSAI OZAKI

winter plum—
flower buds touching
in the faint light

kanbai ya tsubomi fureau hono akari

HIDENO ISHIBASHI

dusky autumn—
for someone yet to come
a single chair

yagate kuru mono ni banshū no isu hitotsu

AKITO ARIMA

autumn night—
the sound of two white plates
touching

shirasara no fureau oto no yoru no aki

YOSHIKO YOSHINO

Such a beautiful beginning to what we're sure will be a beautiful life together. Congratulations! Cynthia and Jimmy Wu

the winter waves:
I can't stop this feeling
could it be love . . .

fuyunami ni omoi yamazaru koi to iuka

KIKUNO INAGAKI

We are so happy! for the two of you! Go Korea + Taiwan :) Love y'all, Jim + Cyn

7

paper dolls:
the look of wanting
to be in love

kamibina ya koi shitasō na kao bakari

SHIKI MASAOKA

8

misty moonlit night—
for faces unbefitting love
there must also be love

oboroyo ya kao ni niawanu koi mo aran

NATSUME SOSEKI

"only one person"
  is noted in the hotel book—
  the cold night

ichinin to chomen ni tsuku yosamu kana

ISSA KOBAYASHI

10

feeling unloved—
I swim out
out to the open sea

ai sarezushite oki toku oyogunari

SHOSHI FUJITA

nights of rain—
lonely, I fall asleep
holding my breasts

samishisa no chibusa daki neru tsuyuyo kana

YOSHIKO YOSHINO

feeling my male body
I toast
a piece of seaweed

waga karada wo kanji tsutsu nori ichimai wo aburi

IPPEKIRO NAKATSUKA

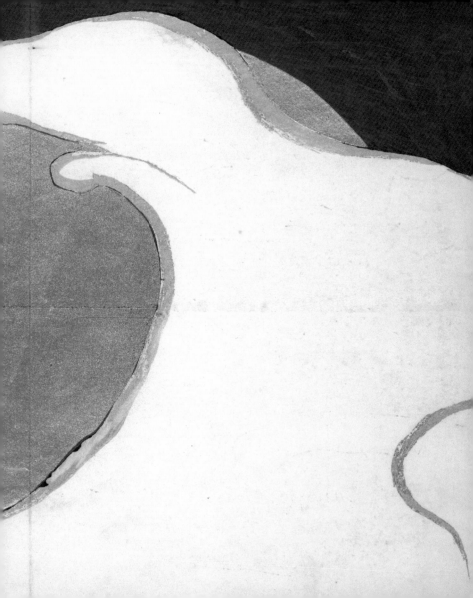

the nape of his neck
draws me in—
moth to flame

higa maeri yoki eriashi wo moteru hito

MASAJO SUZUKI

the soft breathing
of a young woman
this spring afternoon

myōrei no iki shizuka nite haru no hiru

SEISHI YAMAGUCHI

ah, these flower-like faces
make you shy—
the hazy moon

hana no kao ni hareute shite ya oborozuki

BASHO MATSUO

a woman
a woman's body—
the flowering quince

nyonin nyotai yatsude hanasaku

IPPEKIRO NAKATSUKA

the long black hair
of women
blowing in the salty wind

kurokami no nagasa wo shiokaze ni makashi

SANTOKA TANEDA

summer sash—
this slight feeling
of temptation

natsu obi ni honokana uwakigokoro kana

NOBUKO YOSHIYA

going directly
to the one dancing—
and whispering

zukazuka to kite odoriko ni sasayakeru

SUJU TAKANO

stepping around
the moss blossoms—
yearning for someone

koke no hana fumumajiku hito koiiari

TEIJO NAKAMURA

longing to kiss-sip
your round eyes—
autumn mist

tsuburanaru naga me suwanan kiri no aki

DAKOTSU IIDA

24

first love—
faces close
by the stone lantern

hatsu koi ya tōrō ni yosuru kao to kao

TAIGI TAN

Sandra & oliver,
awesome wedding! & you
guys looked amazing.
many blessings on your
marriage! suyeam
&
Jay

25

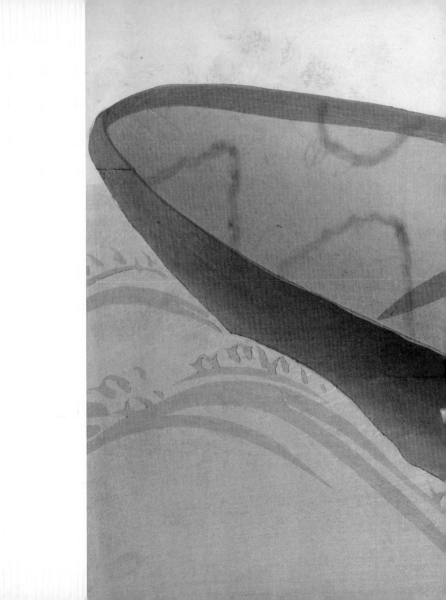

not wanting
to show my heart—
my words in white breath

kokoro misemajiku mono ieba iki shiroshi

TAKAKO HASHIMOTO

28

even while cutting
dried vegetables—
her heart elsewhere

uwaoki no hoshina kizamu mo uwa no sora

YABA SHIDA

spring rain—
in the same carriage
sweet nothings

harusame ya dōsha no kimi ga sazamegoto

TAIGI TAN

the film
ends with a kiss—
coughs everywhere

seppun mote eiga wa tojinu seki michi mitsu

HAKYO ISHIDA

We love you guys
so much! Hope
you really enjoyed
your special day. you're
both beautiful
people.
Love &
Yen &
Suny

divided by a wall—
the murmur of men and women
bathing

kabe wo hedatete yu no naka no danjo sazamekiau

SANTOKA TANEDA

trumpet flowers—
the back room upstairs
in a hot spring's inn

nōzen ya ideyu no yado no ura nikai

SHIKI MASAOKA

wife and child's bedtime—
I stand in the moon-lit
train station

saishira no negoro ya tsuki no eki ni tatsu

RINKA ONO

the awaited one's
distant footsteps
on fallen leaves...

machibito no ashioto tōki ochiba kana

BUSON YOSA

the expected one
enters the small gate—
the key

machibito ireshi komikado no kagi

KYORAI MUKAI

upon returning in deep snow—
I write a letter
to my love

yuki furu naka wo kaerikite tsuma e tegami kaku

SANTOKA TANEDA

pear flowers—
a woman reading a letter
in moonlight

nashi no hana tsuki ni fumi yomu onna ari

BUSON YOSA

40

the first of autumn—
a woman's body glowing...
the dream ends

shinshū ya nyotai kagayaki yume owaru

TOTA KANEKO

thoughts of embracing
my love this spring day—
heading home on a stony path

tsuma dakana shunchū no jari fumite kaeru

KUSATAO NAKAMURA

42

Hey Scolding Companion, Congrats!
—Stan

my scolding companion
if only you were here—
this moon tonight

kogoto iu aite mo araba kyō no tsuki

ISSA KOBAYASHI

43

Oliver &
Sandy,
Congratulations!
Michael / Kari / Lauren / Mikey

snow umbrella—
the sound of closing it,
alone again

yuki no kasa tatamu oto shite mata hitori

MANTARO KUBOTA

choosing
the most exquisite rose—
spring thunder

aekanaru bara erioreba haru no kaminari

HAKYO ISHIDA

What a beautiful
ceremony. What a beautiful
couple. I love you both !!
(but, honestly, Sandra a
bit more.)

45

— Jeannie

is this fragrance

from roses

or from someone passing by?

bara no ka ka ima yukisugishi hito no ka ka

TATSUKO HOSHINO

Oliver & Sandra,
may the Lord bless you
and help you become a sweet
fragrance for Jesus!
we love you!
Pastor Eric &
Lynette

46

I wait in the mist
for my companion
to appear...

kiri no naka ni arawaruru tsure wo machi ni keri

KYOSHI TAKAHAMA

47

PASSION

moonflowers—
the deep folds
begin to open

yūgao ya hiraki kakarite hida fukaku

HISAJO SUGITA

tinged with the blush
of carnal desire—
white peonies

bonnō no beni wo honnori hakubotan

KIYO HINOKI

facing each other
this morning—
as wisteria buds sway

taiza no kokoro fuji no mi no yureteiru asa

IPPEKIRO NAKATSUKA

love's longing—
I place a strawberry
in my mouth

koi shita ya ichigo hitotsubu kuchi ni ire

MASAJO SUZUKI

54

noonday snow—
wiping lipstick
from a Shino tea bowl

yuki no hiru shino chawan ni nokorishi beni nuguu

YOSHIKO YOSHINO

moonflowers—
when a woman's skin
is revealed

yûgao ya onago no hada no miyuru toki

CHIYO-NI

the sultry grass—
and a woman
with voluptuous breasts

kusa ikire nyonin yutakanaru chibusa moteri

IPPEKIRO NAKATSUKA

I just had to sign this page
b/c it contained the word "breasts"!
Ha ha ha! We are so happy for
you guys. With much love
and best wishes. Sam, deeog & QG

snowy window—
the bathing body of a woman
water overflowing

mado no yuki nyotai nite yu wo afureshimu

NOBUKO KATSURA

woman's desire
deeply rooted—
the wild violets

ne wo tsukete onago no yoku ya sumireso

CHIYO-NI

Sandra and Oliver,
Best wishes in
your future. May you
be blessed in many
ways! Nicole +
Jacob

stepping into
the scarlet leaves
for a kiss on the lips

kōyo no naka ni fumiiri kuchi suwaru

YOSHIKO YOSHINO

Sandra & Oliver,
Congrats! We are so
happy for you guys.
We wish you a
wonderful
first yr. together,
Love,
Eric & Liz.

the irises—
I break off a stem
and go to my love

hana ayame hitokuki taoshi aini yuku

KIYOKO UDA

Sandra & Ollie,
congratulations!
Joyce made me
write this,
Kenny

61

my kimono a little loosened—
I meet that someone
this night of fireflies

yuruyaka ni kite hito to au hotaru no yo

NOBUKO KATSURA

Ollie and Sandra,
May much happiness and joy
follow you west.
—Sean

the cave's
drops mingle
into a deep kiss

dōukutsu no shitatari majiru diipu kisu

SUZUKO SHINAGAWA

for whom

is the small pillow...

spring twilight

tagatame no hikuki makura zo haru no kure

BUSON YOSA

66

Written at Keishi's house on the topic of love.

the moon clears—
I accompany a pretty boy
frightened by a fox

tsuki sumu ya kitsune kowagaru chigo no tomo

BASHO MATSUO

a man's burning desire
on an autumn night—
the cranes overhead

shūya hito to moyuru omoi wo tsuru no ue

HAKYO ISHIDA

68

middle age—
ripening in the distance
a night peach

chûnen ya tōku minoreru yoru no momo

SANKI SAITO

the scarlet mushroom:
women adoring it
women rejecting it

akaki take raisan shite wa keru onna

MIKAJO YAGI

aging men
who love men—
the arrowroot flowers

otoko oite otoko wo aisu kuzu no hana

KŌI NAGATA

rainy season—
seaweed entangled close
as lovers

tsuyu no mo yo koishiki mono no gotoku yoru

TAKAKO HASHIMOTO

short summer night—
the sex change operation
is also completed . . .

mijikayo no seitenkan wo itashikeri

MOMOKO TSUJI

fireflies in love:
where the sound of two rivers
come together

koibotaru futatsu no seoto au tokoro

SEISUI SHIIHASHI

sharing this pomegrante
with you—
I split it open

sakeme yori zakuro mafutatsu na to wakatan

TAKEO NAKAJIMA

rendezvous:

entering

a thundercloud

aibiki ga nyūdogumo ni iri yukan

MIKAJO YAGI

Congratulations!
We're so happy for both
of you!

Love,
Jimmy & Grace Kang.

76

rose fragrance—
our first night
folds into whitening skies

bara niou hajimete no yo no shirami tsutsu

SOJO HINO

this flowering night—
a foreign soldier and I
caress fingers

hana no yo ya ikoku no hei to yubi mutsubi

SHIZUKO SUZUKI

in the dark
where you undress
a blooming iris

i wo nugishi yami no anata ni ayame saku

NOBUKO KATSURA

woo hoo!
Congrats!
Love,
Minh + Jen

81

flowery robe
as I undress
sashes coil around me

hanagoromo nugu ya matsuwaru himo iroiro

HISAJO SUGITA

CONGRATULATIONS
SANDRA AND OLIVER!
BEST WISHES ON YOUR MARRIAGE!
Love, BRIAN
+Bridget ♡

82

nights of spring—
tides swelling within me
as I'm embraced

shunya miuchi ni ushio unerite dakare ori

YOSHIKO YOSHINO

soaked
soaked in carnal lust—
the ripe pomegranate

nikkan ni hitari hitaruya ure zakuro

SHIZUKO SUZUKI

Wish you
A
Happy Married
Life
Vijaya & Venkat

84

the fire in my heart
can light
the withered fields

kono kare ni mune no hi hanachinaba moen

KIKUNO INAGAKI

Keven & Juanita Chen
Congratulations on
your big day.

from today
spending nights with a "spouse"
spring dusk

kyo yori no tsuma to tomaru ya yoi no haru

SOJO HINO

Congratulations & Blessings
Oliver & Sandra!
In His grace,
Vic Cheng

86

lovemaking—
a soft rain
surrounds our house

maguwai no shizukanaru ame kyo torimaku

SHIZUKO SUZUKI

Congratulations Oliver & Sandra!
(Oliver, I've been waiting for
this for a long time!)
love,
Jeannie &
Sean

the body arches
at its rainbow peak—
"petite morte"

mi wo sorasu niji no zetten shokeidai

JUSHIN (SHIGENOBU) TAKAYANAGI

rainy cottage—
after lovemaking
the scent of jasmine tea

koi no ato jasumin cha kaoru ame no azumaya

IKUYO YOSHIMURA

shall we die together,
my lover whispers—
evening fireflies

shinouka to sasayakareshi wa hotaru no yo

MASAJO SUZUKI

hard snow—
being embraced
my breath taken away

yuki hageshi dakarete iki no tsumarishi koto

TAKAKO HASHIMOTO

in our robes—
the dark and moonlit nights
of unending love

yukata kite yamiyo tsukiyo to ai tsuzuke

MASAJO SUZUKI

Congratulations Sandra & Olivier!

94

the shadows also
of men and women
dancing . . .

otoko onna to sono kage mo odoru

SANTOKA TANEDA

Congratulations!
We're so happy for you.
May God bless your
marriage abundantly!

Yen + Sunny

under one roof
prostitutes also asleep—
bushclover and the moon

hitotsuya ni yūjo mo netari hagi to tsuki

BASHO MATSUO

Sandra & Oliver
we are praying
for a full & abundant
marriage full of
love!
Love John & Victoria

96

the harbor's
small red-light district—
cotton flowers in bloom

funatsuki no chiisaki kuruwa ya wata no hana

SHIKI MASAOKA

I need the name
of the one standing before me—
night prostitute

yobina hoshi waga mae ni tatsu yoru no shōfu

ONIFUSA SATO

plovers cry—
a woman returns
in the dawn

chidori naku akatsuki modoru onna kana

TAIGI TAN

rose petals scattering—
the sound of my heart
breaking into pieces

bara chiruya onoga kuzureshi oto no naka

TEIJO NAKAMURA

when meeting you now
the painful thorns
in my mouth...

aeba ima kōchu no toge uzuki dasu

SONOKO NAKAMURA

the one I curse
is the one I love—
red cotton roses

norou hito wa sukina hito nari beni fuyō

KANAJO HASEGAWA

no jealousy tonight—
but weeping
over cut onions

shitto nakiyo mo negi kitte namida shite

MIKAJO YAGI

to betray

or to be betrayed—

the shrike's cry

uragiru ka uragiraruru ka mozu takane

MASAJO SUZUKI

letting go
of a slanderous heart
while shelling the beans

hito wo soshiru kokoro wo sute mame no kawa muku

HOSAI OZAKI

half of the mountain
dyed by red maples—
one-sided love

somekanete katayama momiji kataomoi

CHIYO-NI

a pomegranate
opened its mouth—
foolish love affair

zakuro ga kuchi aketa tawaketa koi da

HOSAI OZAKI

tearing up the letter
in the field—
crimson amaryllises

no nite saku fûsho ippen manjushage

NANAKO WASHITANI

if I die of love—
cry at my grave
little cuckoo

koi shinaba waga tsuka de nake hototogisu

OSHU

after our argument:
the two of us gaze at
the golden freesia

kōron no hate furija no ki miru futari

IKUYO YOSHIMURA

Sandra & Oliver,
Congratulations!
May God bless you deeply
through your marriage!

forgiving each other
with only a look—
wisteria in the rain

Love,
Yvonne +
Alice

yurushi au manazashi sumishi fuji no ame

MITSU SUZUKI

113

the morning glory—
like desire
fades away . . .

asagao ya omoi wo togeshi goto shibomu

SOJO HINO

a man reading
a woman sleeping—
the snowy sky

otoko wa yomi onna wa nemuru yukimoyoi

TANIKO TERAI

one in flower

one not—

two poppies in a vase

aru to naki to nihon sashikeri keshi no hana

CHIGETSU

Congratulations, Ollie & Sandra!
    Marriage can be a rough road, but
if you seek God first in your own
spiritual formation, the rewards are incredible.
I pray you will experience God's grace
even more deeply than before. Through
each other. Blessings, Vichi

one stone, and another
nestled together
this moon-lit night

ishi to ishi tsukiyo yorisou

SEISENSUI OGIWARA

117

double rainbow:
the gods and goddesses
have also fallen in love

niji niju kami mo renai shitamaheri

KIYOKO TSUDA

the falling
camellias—
the weight of flesh

ochiru toki tsubaki ni niku no omosa ari

TOSHIRO NOMURA

REMEMBRANCE

Congratulations !
LEVY P.

at the crescent moon
the silence
enters the heart

mikazuki ni hishishi to mono no shizumarinu

CHIYO-NI

123

with a single pillow
I fall asleep tonight
gazing at the fireflies...

hotaru wo mite nemuru yoru no hitotsu no makura

IPPEKIRO NAKATSUKA

124

those nights of love
a dream or illusion?
autumn butterflies

kano koto wa yume maboroshi ka aki no chō

MASAJO SUZUKI

he says a word
I say a word
autumn deepens

kare ichigo ware ichigo aki fukami kamo

KYOSHI TAKAHAMA

holding chopsticks
all alone—
the snow keeps falling

hashi toru ori hata to hitori ya yuki furi furu

TAKAKO HASHIMOTO

in the waves
no trace, where I swam
with a woman

nami ni atokata mo nashi onna to oyogishi ga

SEISHI YAMAGUCHI

128

I turn off the light—
my heart a precipice
before the moon

hi wo kesu ya kokoro gake nasu tsuki no mae

SHUSON KATO

morning cicadas:
all my love and hatred
return to me

semi no asa aizō wa kotogotoku ware ni kaeru

HAKYO ISHIDA

after weeping
my white breath
whiter...

nakishi ato waga shiroiki no yutaka naru

TAKAKO HASHIMOTO

clutching a tissue
she leans
against the sliding door

menugui wo motte shōji ni yorikakari

SONOJO (SONOME)

"Taking leave of Soseki"

for me going
for you staying:
two autumns

yuku ware ni todomaru nare ni aki futatsu

SHIKI MASAOKA

no more waiting
for the evening or the dawn—
touching the old clothes

matsu kure no akebono mo naki kamiko kana

CHIYO-NI

on the dresser
the ring I took off—
cherry blossom rain

kyōdai ni nukishi yubiwa ya hana no ame

MASAJO SUZUKI

135

few words spoken—
husband and wife part
into autumn nightfall

kotoba sukunaku wakareshi fûfu aki no yoi

HISAJO SUGITA

autumn field—
some grasses flower
some grasses don't

aki no no ya hanato naru kusa naranu kusa

CHIYO-NI

is life possible

without regret?

the beer foams over . . .

kui naki sei ari ya biru no awa koboshi

MASAJO SUZUKI

my mate beside me
speaks of the long nights—
I feel it, too

tsuma ga ite yonaga wo ieri so omou

SUMIO MORI

when I eat a persimmon
I think of the one
who loved them

kaki kue ba kaki no suki naru hito omou

MITSU SUZUKI

too far away
for good-byes—
this nakedness

sayonara wo iu ni wa tōki hadaka kana

YATSUKA ISHIHARA

143

my husband's not returning—
I still shine
his mildewed shoes

kaeranedo migakuyo tsuma no kabi no kutsu

SUZUKO SHINAGAWA

moon-lit night—
sleeping beside my loved one
who's dying

gekko ni inochi shiniyuku hito to neru

TAKAKO HASHIMOTO

insects, don't cry—
even lovers and stars
must part

naku na mushi wakaruru koi wa hosi ni sae

ISSA KOBAYASHI

146

my husband gone—
spring snow falls
out of a clear sky

tsuma yuku to seiten haru no yuki wo furu

SHIZUNOJO TAKESHITA

147

snowstorm—
I will die knowing
only a husband's hand

yuki hageshi tsuma no te no hoka shirazu shisu

TAKAKO HASHIMOTO

glad just to test
walking to the kitchen
to be with my wife...

shibo tanoshi kuriya no tsuma ni ai ni yuku

SOJO HINO

149

this world of suffering—
even if the flower opens
even if it opens

ku no shaba ya hana ga hirakeba hiraku tote

ISSA KOBAYASHI

the piercing cold—
in our bedroom stepping
on my dead wife's comb

mi ni shimu ya naki tsuma no kushi wo neya ni fumu

BUSON YOSA

153

wild cherry blossoms—
we part
to meet again

yamazakura wakaruru wa mata awan tame

MOMOKO KURODA

as the old curtain sways
my husband's spirit
returns

sayuragite tsuma yomigaeru furu sudare

SUZUKO SHINAGAWA

tangled white hair
on the wooden pillow—
the chill of night

kimakura ni shirakami nazumu yosamu kana

SEIFU-NI

perfume—
that night, that time
that place

kosui ya sono yo sono toki sono tokoro

HANJO TAKEHARA

at dawn

talking to the flowers

a woman alone

akatsuki no hana ni mono iu hitori kana

SEIFU-NI

old man's love
wanting to forget about it—
winter rain

oi ga koi wasuren to sureba shigure kana

BUSON YOSA

159

the teenage boy—
even at sixty years
a spring-like feeling

shōnen ya rokujûnen go no haru no gotoshi

KŌI NAGATA

while aging—
like a camellia flower
I will still dance

oi nagara tsubaki to natte odori kiri

TAKAJO MITSUHASHI

the statue of Venus—
yet just a large
winter stone

vinasu tari katsu ikkai no fuyu no ishi

AKITO ARIMA

162

the past distant
and more distant
under a radiant sun

toki yo wa urarabi no shita ni nao toki

SHUOSHI MIZUHARA

spring awakening—
my child has read
my love poems

keichitsu ya waga koi no ku wo ko ni yomare

ATSUSHI AZUMI

166

listening to
my grandchild's love stories—
I slice a large melon

mago no koi kiki tsutsu ōki meron kiru

MITSU SUZUKI

spring night—
in bed longing for
the goddess of compassion

haru no yo ya nereba koishi kanzeon

BOSHA KAWABATA

my past fragmented—
yet these cherry blossoms
fall in clusters

kako wa kire gire sakura wa fusa no mama ochite

TAKAKO HASHIMOTO

distant as winter mists—
embracing and
being embraced

fuyumoya no kanata ya daku mo dakareshi mo

MASAJO SUZUKI

even after fallen
the image remains—
the peonies

chirite nochi omokage ni tatsu botan kana

BUSON YOSA

the long life
after our first love—
spring's full moon

hatsukoi no ato no nagaiki haru mangetsu

SUMIKO IKEDA

closing my eyes
I bask in the warmth of love
long past

me o tojite mukashi no koi ni atatamaru

SOJO HINO

Congratulations
Sandra + Oliver!
May each day be filled with
the warmth of Christ's love as it
magnifies in your glowing love for each
other! I pray for constant transparency, in
understanding, forgiveness and love in
your marriage! & Esther Seo

green leaves or fallen leaves
become one—
in the flowering snow

ha mo chiri mo hitotsu utena ya yuki no hana

CHIYO-NI

so many

many ways—

to have been in love

samazama ni shina kawaritaru koi wo shite

BONCHO NOZAWA

Notes

PAGE 8. Shiki was sick with spinal tuberculosis most of his adult life and was bedridden, so he had little chance for romantic love.

PAGE 36. Link #12 from "Summer Moon" *renga* (linked verse), originally from *Sarumino* (The Monkey's Raincoat) linked-verse collection, done with Basho and other haiku poets.

PAGE 54. A note attached to this haiku says, "A round red strawberry makes me think of my first love; after such a long time it might seem strange, but sometimes I feel tempted to fall in love anew."

PAGE 67. This haiku deals with a homosexual love relationship, say the scholars in *Basho and His Interpreters: Selected Hokku with Commentary* by Makoto Ueda (Palo Alto, Calif.: Stanford University Press, 1992), p. 409.

PAGE 96. This is one of Basho's controversial haiku, that he wrote as part of his travel *haibun* (prose and haiku mixed) when he lodged at an inn. The question often asked is: Was he being sympathetic, condescending, or just presenting things as they are?

PAGE 104. A note attached to this haiku says, "There was a difficult period when I thought of being unfaithful to him before he was, but nothing happened after all." She is referring to her lover, not her second husband whom she finally divorced; her true love relationship lasted for forty years.

PAGE 108. This is from a *renga* (linked verse) titled *Himenoshiki* (The Princess Ceremony), done with female poet Shisenjo in 1726; link #27.

PAGE 133. Natsume Soseki (1867–1906) was a novelist and middle school teacher in Matsuyama. When Shiki was leaving Matsuyama for Tokyo, he wrote this haiku for his close friend Soseki.

PAGE 142. Mitsu Suzuki's husband, Zen master Shunyru Suzuki, died in December 1971; this haiku was written for him in the autumn of 1972.

PAGE 146. From Issa's diary entry, this was written when his wife Kiku was dying from an illness. This poem's reference is to the *Tanabata* (star festival) of the weaver star (Vega) and her earth-born lover, the herdsman (Altair); their fate is that they can only meet once a year for one day on the seventh day of the seventh moon in summer.

PAGE 147. This was written shortly after Shizunojo Takeshita's husband died suddenly of a brain hemorrhage in January 1933.

PAGE 149. The last ten years of Sojo Hino's life were spent bed-ridden, his wife nursing him; this haiku reflects a short respite from his illness to see if he could walk to the one he loved.

PAGE 175. Link #31 from "Summer Moon" *renga* (linked verse) originally from *Sarumino* (The Monkey's Raincoat) linked-verse collection, done with Basho and other haiku poets.

About the Poets

AKITO ARIMA (b. 1930). A contemporary male haiku poet; his group's name is *Ten-I* (Providence). Holding various professions including nuclear physicist, past president of Tokyo University, previous minister of education, and president of the Haiku International Association. His own works include *Bokoku*, *Chimei*, and *Risshi*. See translation selections in *Einstein's Century: Akito Arima's Haiku*, translated by Emiko Miyashita and Lee Gurga.

ATSUSHI AZUMI (1907–88). Modern male haiku poet who published in haiku master Sojo Hino's *Kikan* magazine. He later participated in haiku master Mantaro Kubota's group and its magazine, *Shunto* (Spring Lamplight); after Mantaro's death he inherited the magazine. His own collections include *Mazushiki Kyoen*, *Koreki*, and *Gozen Gogo*.

BASHO. See Matsuo, Basho.

BUSON. See Yosa, Buson.

CHIGETSU (1632–1708). Her family name was Kawai. She was the closest woman disciple of Basho, and one of the greatest women haiku poets. After her husband died, she became a Buddhist nun and lived in Otsu with her adopted son, Otokuni, who was also a student of Basho. She was one of the main contributors to the famed *Sarumino* (Monkey's Raincoat) linked-verse collection.

CHIYO-NI (1703–75), or KAGA NO CHIYO. Her family name was Fukumasuya. One of the great traditional women haiku poets. Born into a scroll maker's family, she studied with two of Basho's disciples, and was a renowned *renga* master, painter, and Buddhist nun. She published two poetry books: *Chiyo-ni Kushu* (Chiyo-ni's Haiku Collection) and *Matsu no Koe* (Voice of the Pine). Known for living Basho's "Way of Haiku." See *Chiyo-ni: Woman Haiku Master* by Patricia Donegan and Yoshie Ishibashi.

SHOSHI FUJITA (b. 1926). A contemporary male poet who began as a student of the modern haiku giants Shuoshi Mizuhara and Hakyo Ishida in the 1940s, contributing to their magazine *Ashibi*. He later began his own magazine called *Taka*. His works include *Tojo, Ikko,* and *Kagura*; his essays include *20 Weeks Haiku Guide.*

KANAJO HASEGAWA (1887–1969). She is considered to be one of the great female forerunners of modern haiku. She was originally a student of Kyoshi Takahama, but she later formed her own group and its magazine, *Suimei*. Her works include *Rindo* (Autumn Bellflower) and *Ugetsu* (Moon on a Rainy Night).

TAKAKO HASHIMOTO (1899–1963). One of the great modern women haiku masters, one of the four T's (along with Tatsuko Hoshino, Takajo Mitsuhashi, and Teijo Nakamura) of Japanese haiku. She first learned the koto, but later studied haiku with Hisajo Sugita, Kyoshi Takahama, and Seishi Yamaguchi. Takako was associated with the Hototogisu and Ashibi schools and later with Seishi's *Tenro* (Heaven) school and magazine. Her main works include *Umi Tsubame* (Sea Swallows), *Beniito* (Red Thread), and *Myoju* (The End of Life).

SOJO HINO (1901–56). A modern male haiku poet who was also the editor of two haiku magazines, the seminal *Kikan* (Flagship) and later *Seigen.* He lost much in the air raids of World War II and although bedridden for years, he still produced eight volumes of haiku over his lifetime, among them the famous *Miyako Hotel.*

KIYO HINOKI (b. 1937). A contemporary female haiku poet. She studied with Shugyo Takaha. She heads the *Toyo* (Distant Arrow) haiku group.

TATSUKO HOSHINO (1903–84). One of the famous of the modern female haiku poets, one of the four T's (along with Takako Hashimoto, Takajo Mitsuhashi, and Teijo Nakamura). Tatsuko was a daughter of the famous haiku poet Kyoshi Takahama and was tapped by her father to continue his *Tamamo* (Seaweed) haiku group and magazine.

DAKOTSU IIDA (1885–1962). His pen name was Sanro (Mountain Hut). A Japanese male haiku poet, considered a "modern Basho" because of his adherence to naked nature and a disciplined life. Though he edited a local haiku magazine, *Isinglass,* he spent most of his life as a reclusive poet who lost most of his family in

World War II. Among his works are *Collection of Poems at a Mountain Hut* and *Snowy Valley*.

SUMIKO IKEDA (b. 1936). A contemporary female poet who is a member of *Sendan* and *Ani* haiku groups. Her publications include *Yuki Fune* and *Tamashii no Hanashi*.

KIKUNO INAGAKI (1906–82). A modern female haiku poet who was once an actress. She studied with haiku master Mantaro Kubota and later with Atsushi Azumi. Her collections include *Kaya no mi* (Nuts of the Kaya Tree) and *Toto* (Winter Waves).

HIDENO ISHIBASHI (1909–47). A female haiku poet of modern times who studied with haiku poet Kyoshi Takahama and female tanka poet Akiko Yosano. She was married to haiku critic Kenkichi Yamamoto (1907–88). Her one collection is *Sakura Koku* (Cherry Blossoms Deep). See translations of her work in *Far From the Field: Haiku by Japanese Women*, translated and edited by Makoto Ueda.

HAKYO ISHIDA (1913–69). Modern haiku male poet who was a student of Shuoshi Mizuhara and his modern magazine *Ashibi*

(Staggerbush), but later formed his own magazine, *Tsuru* (Cranes). Although ill for many years with a lung disease, he still managed to write seven volumes of haiku before his death; his best known is *Clinging to Life*.

YATSUKA ISHIHARA (1919–98). A modern male haiku master whose group's name is *Aki* (Autumn). His teachers were Dakotsu Iida and Tatsuji Miyoshi. His haiku theory was "introspective shaping," looking inward as well as outward. His collections include *Shufukin* (Autumn Harmonium), *Danchoka* (Heartbreak Blossoms), and *Hito to Sono Kage* (Person and Shadow). See translations in *Red Fuji*, translated by Tadashi Kondo and William J. Higginson.

ISSA. See Kobayashi, Issa.

TOTA KANEKO (b. 1919). Contemporary male haiku figure of the avant-garde who studied under Shuson Kato. He had a career as a banker besides heading his haiku circle *Kaitei*, and serving as honorary president of the Modern Haiku Association and co-editor (with Kiyoko Uda) of its publication, *The Haiku Universe for the 21st Century: Japanese Haiku 2008 (Japanese and English)*.

His own works include *Topography of the Dark Green Land*, a haiku collection, and *Today's Haiku* on the art of haiku.

SHUSON KATO (1905–93). One of the great modern male haiku poets who was also a Basho scholar. In the 1930s he was associated with the *Ashibi* (Staggerbush) school and magazine founded by Shuoshi Mizuhara, and with its humanist perspective. Later he founded the *Kanrai* (Thunder in Midwinter) journal. His collections include *Maboroshi no Shika* and *Hodaka*; his books on Basho include *Basho Zenku* (Collected Works of Basho).

NOBUKO KATSURA (1914–2004). A prominent female haiku poet of the modern era and student of Sojo Hino. After World War II and the loss of her husband, she worked as a secretary while editing the magazine *Josei Haiku* (Women's Haiku) with Chiyoko Kato. She also founded the magazine *Soen* (Grass Garden). Her works include *Gekko Sho* (Beams of the Moon), *Nyoshin* (The Female Body), and *Kaei* (Shadows of Flowers).

BOSHA KAWABATA (1900–1941). Modern male haiku poet who followed his father as a haiku poet and painter. However, when his father began operating a geisha house, he left home, longing for a hermit's life of meditation. He became bedridden in his twenties and wrote haiku to sustain himself. *The Haiku of Bosha Kawabata: A Definitive Edition*, was published in 1946.

ISSA KOBAYASHI (1763–1828). One of the three greatest traditional male haiku poets, along with Basho and Buson. As a Pure Land Buddhist, he espoused compassion for all living things, perhaps because he himself had a life of poverty and personal tragedy. See his autobiographical haibun collection, *Oraga Haru* (The Spring of My Life) published in 1819.

MANTARO KUBOTA (1889–1963). Modern male haiku poet who was better known as a novelist. He studied with Toyojo Matsune and he participated in a haiku group of artists and writers; later as a haiku master he had his own group and magazine, *Shunto* (Spring Lamplight). His collections include *Michishiba, Kusanoki*, and *Ryugusho*.

MOMOKO KURODA (b. 1938). A contemporary woman haiku poet who studied with master Seison Yamaguchi. She later founded her own group and magazine, *Aoi*. Her main collections include *Ki no Isu* and *Ichhiboku Isso;* her essays include *Momoko Kuroda's Glossary of Season Words.*

SHIKI MASAOKA (1867–1902). One of the four greats with Basho, Buson, and Issa, called "the father of modern Japanese haiku." He created haiku by cutting *hokku* (starting verse) from the longer *renga* (linked verse) and giving it a new name. He was a tanka poet and haiku theorist espousing a "sketch from life." He lived with tuberculosis and died young; his haiku group's magazine was *Hototogisu* (Cuckoo). His works include *A Drop of Ink* and *Haiku Notebook of the Otter's Den*; main disciples include Kyoshi and Hekigodo.

BASHO MATSUO (1644–94). The greatest male haiku poet in Japanese history. Coming from a low samurai class, he became a *renga* master with many disciples, studied Zen, and traveled widely. He took haiku to a deeper level, espousing *haikai no michi* (the Way of Haiku) as a way of life and a return to Nature. See *Sarumino* (The Monkey's Raincoat), a renga collection, and *Oku no Hosomichi* (Narrow Road to the Interior), a haibun collection. See haiku translations in R. H. Blyth's *History* of *Haiku, Vol. 1*, and Makoto Ueda's *Basho and His Interpreters*, among others.

TAKAJO MITSUHASHI (1899–1972). One of the great modern female haiku poets; known as one of the four T's (along with Takako Hashimoto, Tatsuko Hoshino, and Teijo Nakamura). She first wrote haiku under the tutelage of her husband, but then turned to experimental haiku along with other women poets. Collections include *Shida Jigoku* (The Fern Hell) and *Uo no Hire* (Fins of a Fish). Her suffering during World War II produced *Hakkotsu* (The Bleached Bones).

SHUOSHI MIZUHARA (1892–1981). One of the haiku giants of the modern era; known as one of the four S's (along with Seiho Awano, Suji Takano, and Seishi Yamaguchi). He studied with Toyojo Matsune and Kyoshi Takahama. He founded the haiku magazine *Hamayumi* (later known as *Ashibi*) which presented pioneering approaches for modern haiku, diverging from the Hototogisu school. His most known haiku collection is *Katsushika*.

SUMIO MORI (b. 1919). Contemporary male haiku poet whose poetry is known for its humanity. He was a student of Shuson Kato. His own haiku group is *Sugi* (Cedar Tree). His collections include *Shien*, *Kagen*, *Riso*, and *Tenjitsu*; haiku essays include *Mori Sumio Haironshu* (Haiku Criticism).

KYORAI MUKAI (1651–1704). Perhaps the closest of Basho's ten male disciples. Kyorai was the son of a Confucianist and a samurai adept in martial arts and astronomy. Rather than have many students, he preferred to be the disciple, along with Doho, to record Basho's poetic theories in *Haikai Mondo* in 1687, *Tabineron* (Travel Lodging Discussion) in 1699, and *Kyoraisho* (Kyorai's Gleanings) in 1704—all well used by haiku poets since.

KŌI NAGATA (1900–1997). Modern male haiku poet who is also known for his avant-garde *haiga* paintings (pictures with haiku added). His own haiku group and magazine was *Lilaza*. Among his works are *Jinsei* (Life) and *Rani* (High Art). See translations in *A Dream Like This World: One Hundred Haiku by Kōi Nagata*, translated by Nana Naruto and Magaret Mitsutani.

TAKEO NAKAJIMA (1908–88). A modern male haiku poet who was a disciple of Kyoshi and also studied with Sekitei and Shuoshi. He was also a lecturer of Japanese literature and published *Mugi* (Barley) magazine. Collections include *Juyogun* and *Kakoheki*.

KUSATAO NAKAMURA (1901–83). A modern male haiku poet. He studied German literature, and also Japanese literature (especially the haiku poet Shiki), and was a professor at Seikei Gakuen in Tokyo. He founded and led the *Banryoku* (Myriad Green Leaves) haiku group. His works include *The Eldest Son*, *Volcanic Island*, and *Beautiful Fern*.

SONOKO NAKAMURA (1903–2001). A modern female haiku poet who participated in haiku master Mantaro Kubota's group and its magazine, *Shunto* (Spring Lamplight). Later with Shigenobu Takayanagi, she published *Haiku Hyoron* (Haiku Criticism) review magazine. Her collections include *Suiyoshikan*, *Hanagari* (Flower Hunting), and *Ginyu*.

TEIJO NAKAMURA (1900–1988). One of the great modern women haiku masters; known as one of the four T's (along with

Takako Hashimoto, Tatsuko Hoshino, and Takajo Mitsuhashi). In the lineage of Shiki, she studied under Kyoshi who published her haiku in his *Hototogisu* (Cuckoo) magazine. She later had her own movement of women's haiku, as did Kyoshi's daughter, Tatsuko. Teijo's haiku group was *Kazahana* (Snow Flowers in Wind) and her books include *Teijo Haiku Collection* and *Red, White Plum*.

IPPEKIRO NAKATSUKA (1887–1946). One of the truly modern male haiku poets. A student of Hekigodo, he advocated free-verse haiku: often longer, without a 5-7-5 count or a *kigo* (season word). Yet he maintained Basho's humanism. Ippekiro was editor of two modernist haiku magazines: *Kaiko* and *Etude*. His main haiku collection is *1,000 Haiku of Ippekiro*. Later collections are *Pomegranates* and *Cape Jasmine*.

BONCHO NOZAWA (d. 1714). A traditional haiku poet who lived in Kyoto where he worked as a physician. Associated with the Basho circle along with his wife, the haiku poet Uko. His haiku is found in anthologies of the Basho school, including the famous *Sarumino* (The Monkey's Raincoat) renga collection of 1690, which he helped edit.

TOSHIRO NOMURA (1911–2001). A modern male haiku poet who at first participated in the Ashibi group of haiku poet Shuson Kato. Later his own magazine and group was *Oki* (Offshore). Among his works are *Soshakuon* (Chewing) and *Tenjoka* (Flowers of Heaven).

SEISENSUI OGIWARA (1884–1976). One of the male pioneers of free-verse haiku. He broke away from the lineages of Kyoshi—and later haiku poet Hekigodo—to create more subjective haiku. He also formed *Stratus,* the most popular of free-verse haiku magazines. He was married but lived as a Buddhist pilgrim for some years. He was the prolific writer of more than three hundred books of essays, translations from German to Japanese, travel sketches, and haiku.

RINKA ONO (1904–84). A modern male haiku poet who was a pupil of Aro Usuda and then the editor of the magazine *Haiku;* and later editor of his own magazine, *Hamma* (Seashore). Collections include *Kaimon* (Sea Gate) and *Fuyugari* (Winter Geese).

OSHU (seventeenth century). A female haiku poet of Basho's era whose birth and death dates and connection to any haiku school are unknown. She was a courtesan by profession in the licensed quarters. Her poetic gift was so celebrated that some of her verses were included in haiku anthologies of her time.

HOSAI OZAKI (1885–1926). A modern male haiku poet known for his free-verse haiku. He studied with haiku poet Seisensui Ogiwara when young. He later gave up his law practice to become a beggar monk living at temples in Kyoto. Before his only collection of haiku was published, he died of tuberculosis on an island alone in a humble hut. His collection was *Oozora* (Big Sky) written at Sumadera Temple.

SANKI SAITO (1900–1962). Modern male haiku poet who was a part of the New Rising Haiku movement. A dentist in early life, he was introduced to haiku by one of his patients. He helped establish and edit *Tenro* magazine with Seishi Yamaguchi, and later had his own magazine, *Dangai* (Precipice). His collections include *Hata* (Flag), *Kyo* (Today), and *Yoru no Momo* (Night Peach). He helped establish the Modern Haiku Association in 1947.

ONIFUSA SATO (1919–2002). A modern male haiku poet who studied with Sanki Saito and associated with "the new haiku movements" of his times. His own group and magazine is *Kogumaza* (Little Bear Constellation). His collections include *Namonaki Nichiya* and *Segashira*.

SEIFU-NI (1731–1814). Her family name was Enomoto. One of the famous traditional women haiku poets. She belonged to the Basho-revival and was the main female disciple of Shirao Kaya, yet she studied first with Chosui Shirai. She was born into a samurai family and learned haiku from her stepmother. After the death of her husband and later her teacher, Shirao, she became a Buddhist nun at the age of sixty and practiced meditation at a temple in Kamakura. Her son published her collection, *Seifu-ni Kushu.*

YABA SHIDA (1662–1740). One of the famous haiku master Basho's ten male disciples. In 1692 Basho became involved with a new group of Edo poets, centered on Yaba, along with whom he promoted his poetic ideal of *karumi* (lightness). He also helped edit *Sumidawara* (Charcoal Sack), published in 1694, a haiku anthology of the Basho style.

SEISUI SHIIHASHI (1920–2008). A modern male haiku poet who felt that haiku emerges from the inner mind yet is rooted in the seasons—in the tradition of travel haiku poets. He was a senior member of the *Sanreki* (Mountain Calendar) haiku group led by Aoyagi Shigeki.

SUZUKO SHINAGAWA (b. 1932). A contemporary female haiku and renku poet; one of the main disciples of haiku master Seishi Yamaguchi and his *Tenro* (Heaven) circle and magazine. She now heads her own haiku group *Glocke* (German for "Bell"). Among her works are *Suichuka* (Water Flowers), *Hire* (Fins), and *Muka* (Six Fragrances).

SONOJO (SONOME) (1664–1726). Her family name was Shiba. One of the most renowned traditional female haiku poets. Became Basho's student in 1689, and after his death in 1694 she studied with his foremost disciple, Kikaku. She worked as an eye doctor, haiku teacher, and haiku judge, and compiled haiku anthologies. She later became a Buddhist nun.

NATSUME SOSEKI (1867–1916). Known as a famous male novelist and less as a haiku poet. He went abroad to England as a scholar and then worked as a professor of English, but later devoted himself to writing. His first and most famous novel, *I Am a Cat*, was inspired by his friend, the haiku poet Kyoshi Takahama. Although he had much literary success, his later life was tainted by illness.

HISAJO SUGITA (1890–1946). A modern female haiku master. Sugita was a passionate woman who became a leader among women haiku poets of the *Hototogisu* (Cuckoo) school under Kyoshi. She went on to found her own magazine, *Hanagoromo* (Flowered Kimono). She was later dismissed from the Hototogisu school for her eccentricity; she supposedly became insane and died thereafter. After her death, she became more recognized.

MASAJO SUZUKI (1906–2003). One of the modern female haiku poets who focused on love and wrote openly about her forty-year-long love affair. She lived a full life with her circle of poets around the pub-restaurant she ran in Tokyo. She studied mostly with Mantaro Kubota. Her collections include *Unami* (April Waves), *Yubotaru* (Evening Fireflies), and *Shimokuren* (Purple Magnolia). See selected translations in *Love Haiku: Masajo Suzuki's Lifetime of Love*, translated by Emiko Miyashita and Lee Gurga.

MITSU SUZUKI (b. 1914). Most known for being the wife of famous Zen master Shunyru Suzuki; they lived together at the San Francisco and Tassajara Zen Centers in California. Although born in Japan she lived most of her adult life—over thirty years—in America, and now she is back in Japan in her old age. She is a haiku poet and tea ceremony teacher. Her haiku are collected in *Temple Dusk: Zen Haiku*, translated by Kazuaki Tanahashi and Gregory Wood.

SHIZUKO SUZUKI (1919–unknown). A modern female haiku poet whose life is filled with mysterious controversy. A student of Kyoshu Matsumura and his haiku group which published her popular first collection, *Shunrai* (Spring Thunder). In 1950s Occupied Japan, she worked as a dancer near an army base and became involved with an American soldier. Her second collection of haiku, *Yubiwa* (The Ring), reflects her liberated views. She has been classified as a missing person since 1952.

KYOSHI TAKAHAMA (1874–1959). A modern male haiku poet who was the most influential haiku critic of his time and who set up a firm to publish haiku books. He was a prolific writer of haiku (tens of thousands), many of which appear in *Kyoshi Kushu* (Collected Works of Kyoshi), as well as of novels, short stories, and essays. After his teacher Shiki's death, as a main disciple, Kyoshi took over *Hototogisu* (Cuckoo), which is still carried on by his granddaughter, Teiko Inahata (b. 1930).

SUJU TAKANO (1893–1976). A modern male poet, one of the male haiku greats of the twentieth century known as the four S's (along with Seiho Awano, Shuoshi Mizuhara, and Seishi Yamaguchi). He began his career as a university professor of medicine, but under the urging of Shuoshi Mizuhara, Suju started contributing haiku to *Hototogisu* magazine. He later founded his own school, *Seri*. His haiku collections include *Hatsu Garasu* and *Yakashu*.

JUSHIN (SHIGENOBU) TAKAYANAGI (1923–83). An avant-garde modern male haiku poet who was influenced by French modernist literature. He studied with Kakio Tomizawa and cofounded the magazine *Bara*, which he edited among others, like the *Haiku Kenkyu* (Haiku Study) magazine. Known for his symbolic and somewhat erotic haiku, and also his experiments with one- and four-lined haiku. Among his works are *Sankaishu* and *Complete Works of Shigenobu Takayanagi*.

HANJO TAKEHARA (1903–98). Modern female haiku poet who was better known for dance and the promotion of Japanese arts. One of the greatest dancers of traditional Japanese dance. Yet she also studied haiku with the famous haiku poet Kyoshi Takahama. Her real first name was Han but her haiku name was Hanjo. Her collections include *Takehara Han Ichidai* (The Life of Takehara Han) and *Hanju*.

TAIGI TAN (1709–71). Although he is not so known, he is considered to be one of the great male haiku poets, on par with his friend Buson. He was a poet of the Edo School of haiku in the Kikaku (a disciple of Basho) lineage, which placed more emphasis on people rather than nature. He entered the Zen priesthood for a while but gave it up and lived in the "gay" quarters of Shimabara where he taught haiku, tutored children, and enjoyed life.

SANTOKA TANEDA (1882–1940). One of the eccentric modern male haiku poets. He was rescued from a suicide attempt when young and went on to become one of the last Zen pilgrim-monks of the twentieth century. His haiku was as free-style as his life; he used the principle of the haiku spirit, but not the form of any set syllable count or *kigo* (season word). See translations in *Mountain Tasting: Zen Haiku* by Santoka Taneda, translated by John Stevens.

SHIZUNOJO TAKESHITA (1887–1951). A modern female haiku poet who balanced her five children with a career as a teacher, librarian, and haiku poet. She was a part of the Hototogisu circle led by Kyoshi—and was the first woman to be given a place on the opening page of his magazine. She later created her own group, the Students Haiku League with its magazine *Seisoken*. Her collection is *Hayate* (The Gusty Wind).

TANIKO TERAI (b. 1944). A contemporary woman haiku poet who heads her own group and magazine, *Jimeisho*. She has been the previous vice president of the Modern Haiku Association. Her publications include *Jinkan* and *Shiki o Miru* (Looking at Shiki).

KIYOKO TSUDA (b. 1920). A contemporary female haiku poet who began as an elementary school teacher and later became a student of haiku masters Takako Hashimoto and Seishi Yama-guchi. She founded her magazine *Sara* (Sala Tree) and later her own group and magazine, *Kei* ("K"). Her own collections include *Raihai* (Worship) and *Juso* (Mountaineering).

MOMOKO TSUJI (b. 1945). A contemporary female haiku poet who studied with Kenkichi Kusumoto and Soha Hatano. She now has her own magazine, *Doji*. Her collections include *Momo* (Peach), *Hana* (Flower), and *Hirugao* (Moonflower); her haiku essay is entitled *Haiku Ite Tanoshi* (Haiku Is a Pleasure).

KIYOKO UDA (b. 1935). A contemporary female haiku poet whose teacher was Nobuko Katsura with her group *Soen* (Grassy Garden). She is the current president of the Modern Haiku Association. Her haiku collections include *Rira no Ki* (Lilac Tree), *Natsu no Hi* (Summer Days), and *Hanto* (Peninsula). She is the co-author of *Joyru Haiku Shusei* (Collected Works of Women's Haiku), and the co-editor with Tota Kaneko of *The Haiku Universe for the 21st Century: Japanese Haiku 2008 (Japanese and English)*.

NANAKO WASHITANI (b. 1923). A contemporary female haiku poet who participated in *Ashibi* (Staggerbush) magazine led by

Shuoshi. She studied with Sodo Yamaguchi and inherited his group and magazine, *Nanpu* (South Wind). Her haiku collections include *Osai, Jushin*, and *Yuei.*

MIKAJO YAGI (b. 1924). A modern female haiku poet known for her avant-garde experimental *zen'ei* haiku style. She studied first with Suzuka Noburo in the *shasei* (sketch) haiku style and later with Seito Hirahata and Sanki Saito of the New Rising Haiku movement. She was also an active feminist and promoter of the female poet Akiko Yosano's work. Her works include *Benitake* (The Scarlet Mushroom) and *Shigo* (Personal Conversation).

SEISHI YAMAGUCHI (1901–94). One of the male haiku giants of the twentieth century known as the four S's (along with Seiho Awano, Shuoshi Mizuhara, and Suji Takano). He was a disciple of Kyoshi, who was a disciple of Shiki, the father of modern haiku. Seishi advocated modern themes and "an imagination jump," but adhered to the 5-7-5 form and *kigo* (season word). His group and magazine, *Tenro* (Heaven), flourish today. His collections include *Toko* (Frozen Harbor) and *Setsugaku* (Frozen Peak). See *The Essence of Modern Haiku: 300 Poems by Seishi*, translated by Takashi Kodaira and Alfred Marks.

BUSON YOSA (1716–84). One of the three greatest traditional male haiku and renga poets (along with Basho and Issa), Buson was also a painter of the literati art style and a master of elegant images; he also illustrated Basho's haiku. He was a student of Hajin, a close disciple of Kikaku (Basho's disciple). He later promoted the "back-to-Basho revival" that restored haiku to its former state. Some works include *Ake Garasu* (A Crow at Dawn) and *Shin Hanatsumi* (New Flower Picking).

IKUYO YOSHIMURA (b. 1944). Her pen name is Ikumi. A contemporary female haiku poet who is a professor of English. She has a keen interest in American Beat poets who were influenced by Japanese haiku, and has written essays on haiku in English. She is head of the writing circle Evergreen. She publishes in haiku magazines, both Japanese and international; her works include *Spring Thunder, Honeysuckle,* and *Renaissance of the Works of R. H. Blyth.*

YOSHIKO YOSHINO (b. 1915). A contemporary female poet who often writes about love as well as nature. She is from Matsuyama, birthplace of Shiki, the father of modern haiku. She joined the haiku group *Hama* (Seashore) led by Rinka Ono, but formed her own group and magazine, *Hoshi* (Star), that is involved with international haiku. Her main collections include *Hatsuarashi* (White Camellias) and *Ryusui* (Flowering Water), and her work is found in *Tsuru* (Cranes) translated by Emiko Miyashita and Lee Gurga.

NOBUKO YOSHIYA (1876–1973). Modern female haiku poet who was better known as a popular novelist of her time. Her teacher was famous haiku poet Kyoshi Takahama. She also published in Hakyo Ishida's haiku magazine.

Index of Poets

LIBRARY OF CONGRESS CATALOGING-IN-PUBLICATION DATA

Love haiku: Japanese poems of yearning, passion, and remembrance /
[edited by] Patricia Donegan, with Yoshie Ishibashi.—1st ed.

p.   cm.

Includes index.

ISBN 978-1-59030-629-1 (alk. paper)

1. Haiku—Translations into English. 2. Love poetry, Japanese—Transla-
tions into English. I. Donegan, Patricia. II. Ishibashi, Yoshie.

PL782.E3L67 2010

895.6'104108—dc22

2009024130